Facilitator's Guide

What Great Teachers Do *Differently* DVD

Todd Whitaker

EYE ON EDUCATION
6 DEPOT WAY WEST, SUITE 106
LARCHMONT, NY 10538
(914) 833–0551
(914) 833–0761 fax
www.eyeoneducation.com

10 9 8 7 6 5 4 3 2 1

Editorial and production services provided by
Hypertext Book and Journal Services
738 Saltillo St., San Antonio, TX 78207-6953 (210-227-6055)

Table of Contents

Introduction

"Teaching is the profession that makes all other professions possible".

You have chosen a profession that provides the foundation for student to excel in their learning. Schools and education are the equalizers for individuals to rise above personal circumstances and achieve their goals and dreams.

What are you doing to help students learn? Are you one of the "great teachers" that will be discussed in the video? If yes—Congratulations! You can help others in your school wanting to be great. If no—then this video can help you professionally and personally in making the changes needed to move you toward becoming a "great teacher"

In a time of high national and state expectations for school achievement, schools must determine how to meet these expectations. "People—not Programs" are the key to success and those schools that focus on developing "great teachers" will see students succeeding at higher levels. Utilizing the ideas and concepts found in the video is a critical first step toward "greatness."

Dr. Todd Whitaker, through his insight and presentation, will walk you through what traits and characteristics make a "great teacher." This video is not about a program but a chance to determine how effective you are and how you can improve yourself and your student's achievements.

Note to Facilitators: This Facilitator's Guide can be utilized for professional development with staff or as a roadmap for Individual Professional Growth goals. There are guided questions for both group discussions and for individual self-reflection and goal setting.

Eye on Education would like to thank Nancy Satterfield, Assistant Superintendent, Professional Development, Henderson County School District, Henderson, Kentucky, for her assistance in the preparation of the Facilitator's Guide.

If you want to **Go Further** and order a copy of the Guide for each member of your group who will be watching the video, multiple copy discounts apply:

10 - 24 copies –	5% discount
25 - 74 copies –	10% discount
75 - 99 copies –	15% discount
100 - 199 copies –	20% discount
200 - 299 copies –	25% discount
300 - 399 copies –	30% discount
More?	Call **888-299-5350**

Chapter 1:
The Standard of Greatness

Key Concepts

1. Your community and parents expect great schools and great teachers working with their students.
2. Great Principals focus on the growth of their teachers and help them develop to their fullest potential.
3. Everyone in the building should be considered a teacher regardless of the position they hold.
4. Everyone in the building should be considered a leader regardless of the position they hold.
5. The Leadership Tree—How do you identify your Leadership Skills?

Key Concept 1

Communities and parents expect to send their students to great schools.

After hearing Dr. Whitaker on the video, answer the following questions either with a group or individually.

Discussion Questions:

1. How would you rate your school—Great, Good, Needs to Improve?

2. On what factors do you base your school rating?

3. Can this rating be improved? How can it be accomplished?

4. Have you/your school formally or informally asked for feedback from your parents or community in determining how the school is perceived?

5. How do you feel the parents and community would rate your school today?

Reflection/Comment Summary: What can you personally do to make your school/classroom better?

Remember: **Great schools begin with great people. Do your best to be one of the great teachers in your school.**

Key Concept 2

Great Principals focus on the growth of their teachers and help them develop to their fullest.

Dr. Whitaker discussed the need for principals to focus on the people in their building and why it's people—not programs, that can make a difference in a school. Discuss the questions in a group or answer individually.

Discussion Questions:

1. Dr. Whitaker talked about programs schools adopt such as "Assertive Discipline" and the factors needed to make it a success. Think of a program your school has adopted. Did it work as anticipated? If yes—what were the factors that made it successful. If no—what were the factors that led to its less than anticipated results.

List the pros and cons of your identified program.

____

____

____

____

____

____

2. How can your principal best support you in improving your classroom instruction and management?

____

____

____

____

____

____

Reflection/Comment Summary: How can you best help yourself to improve your classroom instruction and management? List at least one area you would like to improve and make a plan for the steps you will take to make the changes happen. Implement the plan and reflect on the success of your efforts.

Area to improve:

____

____

____

____

____

____

____

____

____

____

____

What I will do:

____

____

____

____

____

____

____

____

____

____

____

What criteria will I use to determine change has occurred:

Reflect on the changes I implemented and how they impacted my classroom:

Remember: Great Principals help their staff to be Great Teachers and by working together—Great Results will follow.

Key Concept 3

Dr. Whitaker stated that everyone in the school can be considered a teacher—regardless of the role they have in the school. This means that secretaries, clerks, custodians, food service workers, and others influence the students in the building and all should be held to a high level of behavior expectations. All staff should understand their responsibility toward providing a positive school culture and promoting a safe environment for the students.

Discussion Question:

1. Do all of your staff members feel they are part of the "teaching team"? What ways can they contribute to teaching students appropriate behaviors within their respective areas?

Staff Position:

____

What can they do to assist students?

____

____

____

____

Staff Position:

____

What can they do to assist students?

____

____

____

____

Key Concept 4

Dr. Whitaker stated that everyone in the school can be considered a leader—regardless of the role they have in the school. As with the role of teacher, discuss the implication for leadership from all staff members.

Discussion Question:

1. Do all your staff members feel they are part of the "leadership" in the school? What are ways they can contribute to being positive leaders within their role in the school?

Staff Position:

____

What can they do to be positive leaders?

____

____

____

____

____

____

Staff Position:

____

What can they do to be positive leaders?

____

____

____

____

____

____

Compile a master list of suggestions within your group and compare suggestions/ideas. Make a plan to work with all staff in helping them understand their roles and responsibilities within the school in providing assistance to students through their behaviors and actions.

Remember: Great Schools have ALL staff working together for the benefit of their students.

Key Concept 5

The Leadership Tree

Below is a picture that depicts children on various branches of a tree. Study the tree and decide which figure best represents you and your leadership role within your school.

I chose the figure

____

____

If feel this figure best describes my leadership style because ...

____

____

____

____

Please comment on the selections of other people in your group regarding the figures in this drawing which represent their leadership styles.

Staff members will see that regardless of where they think they are on the Leadership Tree—everyone plays a role in helping the school to be successful. You should also see that there is always room to move up the ladder of leadership to new roles and responsibilities.

Chapter 2: Coming Across to Others

Key Concepts

1. Teacher perception by staff, students, and parents
2. Teacher Behavior Choices
3. Self-Evaluation

Key Concept 1

Understanding your effectiveness is a critical indicator of a great teacher. This concept may by one of the most important to be discussed in this manual as your effectiveness as a teacher leads to any and all improvements in your school and your students' learning. **Effective teachers are the key to all student achievement.**

Discussion Questions/Self-Reflection:

1. Dr. Whitaker states that great teachers know their effectiveness in teaching and classroom management. Think back to a recent classroom instructional time. How would you determine if all your students were engaged in the lesson?

____

____

____

____

2. What did you do if they weren't?

____

____

____

____

3. What can you do if you feel you need help in addressing a weak area in your teaching?

____

____

____

____

4. Think about a lesson that didn't go quite as well as you planned. Describe the lesson weakness.

5. Determine what you think could have been improved/changed to make the lesson more engaging and improve the outcome. Describe what could have been done differently.

6. Incorporate those ideas for change in an upcoming lesson. Then come back and record how you think your teaching method improved.

7. Share your experience with a colleague or your principal.

Remember: A Great School is full of effective teachers who know how to teach to reach all students.

Key Concept 2

Teacher behavior choices set the tone for learning in their classrooms, for professional relationships with colleagues, and with effective communication with parents.

Discussion Questions/Self-Reflection:

1. How would you describe yourself in terms of your classroom behavior?

2. What would a colleague or your principal describe if they were to observe your classroom?

3. Do you feel you are always positive when working with your students? Give examples.

4. Do you have any area you might need to work to improve? Give examples.

Remember: Great Teachers model positive behaviors and have high expectations for themselves as well as for their students.

Key Concept 3

Dr. Whitaker feels that the biggest difference in more effective teachers and less effective teachers is their ability to understand how they come across to others. How your teaching is perceived by your students, parents, and colleagues must be understood before teachers can work to improve.

On earlier pages you described what you think are your best qualities as a teacher. Review those for a moment.

Discussion Questions/Self-Reflection:

Answer the following questions as truthfully as you can:

1. What do I believe are my strengths as a teacher?

____

____

____

____

____

____

____

2. What do I believe I should improve?

____

____

____

____

____

____

____

3. A difficult task is to ask others how you are perceived in your teaching.

The following surveys can be given to your students (all or a representative sample that you feel will give you honest feedback) and to some or all of your colleagues to determine how you are seen in their eyes.

List the feedback you received from the student's questionnaire regarding:

Strengths:

Areas to improve:

4. Note the feedback you received from your colleague's questionnaire regarding:

Strengths:

Areas to improve:

Remember: A Great Teacher has the ability to know how they come across to their students and is always working to improve their effectiveness.

Student Questionnaire

As a student in my classroom:

What would you describe are my strengths as a teacher?

If you were talking to me about our class:

What would you suggest I do to improve our class?

Colleague Questionnaire

As a colleague who I have worked with:

What do you believe are my strengths as a teacher?

What could you suggest I do to improve my teaching?

Chapter 3:
Why Do We Care About Great?

Key Concepts

1. We can only learn from Effective people
2. It's People—Not Programs
3. Accept Responsibility for Improving
4. Tone and Manner
5. Confidence—A valuable gift

Key Concept 1

We can only learn from effective people. Dr. Whitaker feels that educators who want to be great teachers find value in examining what effective teachers do that less effective teachers do not.

Discussion Questions:

1. Think of a great teacher you had when you were in school. Describe what the teacher/classroom was like.

____

____

____

____

____

____

____

____

____

____

____

____

____

____

____

2. Underline the adjectives you used to describe that teacher/classroom.

3. Share your list of adjectives with a colleague/team and compile a list of characteristics you used to describe that teacher/classroom.

4. Do you exhibit many of those same characteristics in your classroom? Reflect on what you think you do similarly to your favorite teachers and an area you could work to improve.

5. Pick one area you would like to improve and incorporate it into your lesson activities within the next week. Describe what you plan to do.

6. *One week later.* Describe the impact this activity had in your classroom.

7. If it was positive—will you continue it? If yes—share your success with a colleague.

Remember: Effective teachers learn from other effective teachers. Use the strengths of your colleagues to learn and grow into a great teacher.

Key Concept 2

It's People—Not Programs that make a difference in our schools. Dr. Whitaker stated that programs are only as effective as the people who are to implement them. The only way to improve schools is to either get better teachers or improve the teachers we have in the schools.

The discussion points and reflection questions in the previous chapters were designed to facilitate what a great teacher does and accomplishes in their classrooms. This concept of People—Not Programs is focusing on what you can do to improve yourself as a teacher.

Based on your ideas and thoughts from the previous pages—select one or two areas you would like to focus on to improve your teaching. Classroom instruction or management issues, organization, personal relationships with students, discipline, or other topics are areas most teachers can work to improve.

Topic Selected:

____

Steps I will take to research this area to find evidence of "best practice"

____

____

____

____

____

____

____

____

____

____

____

____

Timeline for implementation:

____

Indicators/criteria I will use to determine successful implementation:

____

____

____

____

____

____

____

____

The outcome of my effort toward change:

____

____

____

____

____

____

____

____

This is a valuable way to take responsibility for improving your ability to teach students to higher levels than before. Either by working alone or with a colleague(s), you will incorporate the "best practices" that have been proven to be successful.

Remember: It's how you do what you do that makes the difference in your classroom.

Key Concept 3

Teachers must accept responsibility for improving. This concept adds to the previous concept by again highlighting the need for teachers to accept personal responsibility for what occurs in their classrooms day in and day out. Dr. Whitaker discussion focused on the idea that the main variable in the classroom is the teacher.

Discussion Question/Self-Reflection:

1. Do you agree with the statement that it's the teacher—not the programs, students, parents, or other factors that determine the success of students in achieving?

List your discussion points:

Share your thoughts with your group.

2. An example Dr. Whitaker used on the video is the question—If your students do poorly on an assignment—who is to blame? Who does Dr. Whitaker feel is to blame? Do you agree or disagree?

List your discussion points:

Share your thoughts with your group.

3. Who is responsible for ensuring that students understand the concepts/ideas within a lesson?

4. What can be done to ensure that students learn?

Share your ideas with your group. Compile a list your group generates to study and gain ideas from each other on how to improve your teaching.

Remember: We are the one variable that we have control over in our efforts to improve.

Key Concept 4

Great Teachers know it's all about your tone and manner. Have you ever had anyone tell you "it's not what you said but the way you said it that got you in trouble." The tone and manner of speaking that a teacher uses sets the climate for their classroom.

Discussion Question/Self-Reflection:

1. Dr. Whitaker talks on the video about how some students don't know how to respond because they've never been taught the right way. The manner in which a teacher talks to their students gives students a model that students will learn from. Which kind of model do you employ in your classroom?

2. What terms/adjectives would you use to describe how a teacher speaks in an effective classroom?

Share your terms/ adjectives with your team/others.

3. Is your list consistent with "best practice" when speaking to students? If yes—great. If not—what can you do to improve?

Remember: It's often not what you say—but how you say it—that influences the outcome of a conversation.

Key Concept 5

Dr. Whitaker stated that confidence is a valuable gift that a principal can give a teacher and that a teacher can give a student.

Discussion Questions/Self-Reflection:

1. What does that statement mean to you?

2. Think of examples when someone has shown confidence in you/your ability to do something.

3. How did it make you feel?

4. Can you think of an example of when you expressed confidence in a student to encourage them? What was the outcome?

5. Do you use confidence building as a technique to help your students succeed? If yes, describe your examples and share them with your team/others.

6. Compile the team's list and share it with everyone so others can effectively try to incorporate confidence building within their classrooms.

Remember: Believing in your students can help them believe in themselves.

Chapter 4: Random versus Plandom

Key Concepts

1. Random versus Plandom
2. High Expectations for Yourself and your students
3. Prevention rather than revenge

Key Concept 1

A great teacher's classroom is well planned and organized for learning. Nothing happens randomly or without purpose.

Discussion Questions/Self-Reflection:

1. Random or Plandom: How would you describe your planning and organizational skills in terms of your room, your lessons, and your activities for your students?

2. Too often, teacher lesson plans only outline pages to be covered or the questions to be answered at the end of the chapter. Do your plans include the expected level of learning that you expect your students to know/be able to do? If yes, give examples.

If not, what can you do to improve your lesson plans to clearly outline the learning that should occur?

Notes

3. As you write your next set of lesson plans—include what level of learning you expect your students to achieve. Provide your students with the expected outcomes through a rubric defining what they should know and/ or be able to do following the lesson. (Example—Your students will be assigned to write an article to the newspaper explaining an activity your school is sponsoring. You should define what an article to be published should include; give examples of well-written articles; and give samples of writings that fall within the different levels of the rubric)

Following the implementation of this lesson—reflect on what worked well, what didn't work, and how the lesson could be refined for the future.

Remember: Great Teachers always have a plan for learning in their classrooms.

Key Concept 2

Great teachers have High Expectations for themselves as well as for their students.

Discussion Questions/Self-Reflection:

1. Dr. Whitaker talked about having High Expectations for yourself as well as your students. What does that mean to you?

2. Share your thoughts with a colleague or team members.

3. Compile a Personal High Expectations list for you to consider and review. Evaluate which of the descriptors you feel could be representative of you. List those:

4. Do you feel you have high expectations for your students? Describe what you do to convey your high expectations to your students and how you help them meet your expectations.

Remember: Great Teachers always have a plan for learning in their classrooms.

Key Concept 3

Great Teachers focus on prevention rather than revenge. Dr. Whitaker discussed the need for teachers to work on preventing those behaviors you don't want in your classroom rather than having to deal with consequences for misbehaviors.

Discussion Questions/Self-Reflection:

1. How do you/your school convey school rules/behavior expectations to your students?

2. Do you spend the time when needed to teach students the behaviors you expect?

3. List options you have when a student misbehaves in your classroom.

4. Share your list with your group. As a group, discuss which options always seem to be the most effective. Highlight the "best options."

5. Determine which of the "best options" you want to use when working with misbehaving students. Try it for a two-week period and then reflect on how it worked for you.

6. If it wasn't as successful as you had planned—select another "best option" from the list and try it. Teachers must constantly work to find the strategies/techniques that will help them be effective.

7. Describe the ideal way you want your class to be conducted each day?

8. Is this a description of your class? If yes—Great. If no, reflect on what you want to change in your classroom to maximize learning.

9. Steps to improve your classroom management could include: (1) Research proven classroom management techniques, (2) ask your principal for help, or (3) ask to observe someone in your building who has good classroom management.

10. Do you feel you have high expectations for your students? Describe what you do to convey your high expectations to your students and how you help them meet your expectations.

11. Set a timeline for implementation of the new idea.

12. Reflect on how the technique worked and what the next steps will be.

Remember: Learning can not take place in an ineffectively managed classroom.

Chapter 5: Ten Days Out of Ten

Key Concepts

1. Great Teachers:

   Never Argue

   Never Yell

   Never Use Sarcasm

2. Teach Appropriate Behaviors and Responses

Key Concept 1

Great Teachers do not utilize arguing, yelling, or sarcasm when working with their students. Teachers should address all students as if they were talking to the best students in their class/school.

Discussion Questions/Self-Reflection:

1. Dr. Whitaker stated that great teachers never argue with their students but teach appropriate responses. Describe several ways you can teach appropriate responses to your students.

Situation:

Response to teach:

Situation:

Response to teach:

2. Share your list with your colleagues and compile a master list of techniques everyone could incorporate into their classrooms.

3. Select a technique from this list you would like to use more often in your classroom.

4. Implement this technique for a two-week period. Reflect on how it worked for you.

5. Share your experience with others on how this technique impacted your classroom.

6. The second behavior caution discussed was the need to never yell in your classroom. Have you ever walked down a hallway and heard a teacher's voice coming from several doors down as they berate their whole classroom for something that occurred? How did it make you feel to hear it?

____

____

____

____

7. How do you think the class felt?

____

____

____

____

8. Dr. Whitaker stated that decisions should be based on your best students. How do you think the best students felt being yelled at about something they more than likely didn't do?

____

____

____

____

9. Have you ever punished the whole class for the actions of one or two? (ex. Someone threw a pencil across the room and hit a student but you don't know who did it and no one will confess. So you make the students all stay in from recess until you find out who the culprit was.) How did the class respond?

____

____

____

____

10. How do you think the students not involved feel about the punishment?

11. In thinking back on such a situation—could you have handled it differently? Discuss with your colleagues a situation and brainstorm other solutions to try so that you are prepared if the situation occurs again.

12. Make a list of other scenarios and possible solutions.

The third cautionary behavior stressed was not to use sarcasm in the classroom as a means of addressing students. Dr. Whitaker defined sarcasm as humiliation under the guise of humor.

13. Ineffective teachers use sarcasm as a means to try and control students by embarrassing them in front of their peers. Often students will remain quiet in a class for fear of answering incorrectly and being subjected to a sarcastic reply. Can you think of a teacher from your past that used sarcasm in their classroom?

____

____

____

____

14. How did the sarcastic comments make you feel—even if they weren't directed at you?

____

____

____

____

15. Reflect on your classes during the past week or two. Have you used sarcastic comments with your students? If yes—think of how you can prevent this type of response in the future.

____

____

____

____

Remember: Teachers never know how their actions and words will influence students now and into their future.

Chapter 6: Thinking Through Decisions

Key Concepts

1. Three Questions to consider when making a decision:

   What is the Purpose?

   Will this accomplish the purpose?

   What do the best people think?

Key Concept 1

Dr. Whitaker stated in the video that teachers should filter their decisions through three primary questions. These questions are used in everything from determining class assignments to class expectations and should be based on your best students.

Discussion Questions/Self-Reflection:

1. When you give an assignment to your students—you hopefully have a reason to do so. However, do you also define the "purpose" of the assignment? Do you explain to your students why they are doing the assignment and what learning should take place? Reflect on your response and write your thoughts.

2. Reflect on recent assignments you gave your classes. Do you think your students knew the "purpose" for the assignment? If yes, describe why you think they did.

3. Discuss with your colleagues the difference between "a reason for the assignment" and "the purpose of an assignment." This discussion can also include topics such as the reason versus purpose for grades, homework, class assignments, tests, etc. List your discussion points.

Notes

4. A second filter in making decisions is to ask yourself "Will this accomplish the purpose?" Will what you are asking the students to do get them to the expected outcome? Based on your reflection and discussion regarding "What is the Purpose," do you think there is a direct connection between your assignment's purpose and the level of understanding that was to be accomplished? Explain why or why not.

5. Another example Dr. Whitaker used in the video is the placement of signs in the school (limit 20 copies) or what you find in stores (Shoplifters WILL be Prosecuted). Who are the signs meant for? What was the purpose of the signs?

6. Do you think they will accomplish the purpose? Why or why not?

7. The third filter is the question "What do the Best People Think" and Dr. Whitaker feels you should base your decisions on that factor. What do you think the best people feel about the copy limit signs, the shoplifting signs, the assignments, etc.?

8. Look around your classroom/school and see if there are examples similar to the copy limits, memos coming around to all teachers, etc. Could there be a different approach to getting the message across? What would you suggest?

9. Discuss it with your colleagues/team and compile a list of alternative ways to address those issues.

10. Before assigning class work/homework the next time—ask your best students for input into the development of an effective learning assignment. The student's suggestions were:

11. Reflect on how successful you feel their suggestions were in getting the work completed and understood to the level of learning you set.

Remember: Put the emphasis on your best staff and students when determining your decisions.

Chapter 7: You are the Filter

Key Concepts

1. Positive or Negative—Which are You?
2. Teachers set the tone in their classrooms.
3. Focus on your challenges in a positive manner.

Key Concept 1

Positive or Negative Attitude. Which best describes you? Dr. Whitaker talked about Great Teachers having a positive attitude toward their students and their job and the influence their attitude has in their classroom.

Discussion Questions/Self-Reflection:

1. What qualities comprise a positive attitude?

2. Share your list with your colleagues.

3. Identify those qualities you feel you possess.

4. List at least four techniques you use to keep your classroom focused on learning.

5. Share these techniques with your group and discuss how these positively impact your teaching. Compile a list of everyone's techniques to use when needed.

6. Many teacher workrooms/lounges should have signs stating "Toxins Spilled Hourly" due to the negative energy spilling out of them. If you think this could describe your workroom/lounge, brainstorm how you/your colleagues can reverse the climate.

7. Ideally, the workroom should be an area of collegial support and a time to refocus before your next class or plan for new learning experiences for your students. If that is not the case—what can be done to help set up such an area.

Remember: Focusing on a developing a positive attitude and filtering out the negative responses can help create a successful classroom and school environment.

Key Concept 2

Teachers establish the tone of our classrooms and students respond to what we model.

Discussion Questions/Self-Reflection:

1. Have you ever walked into someone's classroom and you wanted to stay there all day because of the "feeling" in the classroom? What can make a classroom a "welcoming" room?

2. Do you think a room's atmosphere is indicative of the teaching that is occurring in there? If yes—list some examples to support your belief.

3. What feeling do you get when you walk into a classroom that has absolutely nothing on the walls or no materials for the students to use? What is the "tone" of that class?

4. Research has shown that classrooms must support learning through the multiple intelligences. What does that mean to you and your content area/ grade level?

5. Reflect on your classroom from both the physical environment and the manner in which you speak to and with your students. Have you established a positive classroom culture?

6. What can you do differently if the classroom culture is not as positive as you would like?

Remember: A positive, inviting classroom can set the tone for learning.

Key Concept 3

Focus on your challenges in a positive manner. Teaching may be one of the most pressure filled jobs anywhere. But how you respond to the challenges can determine your effectiveness as a teacher and how well your students will learn. Dr. Whitaker stated that constant griping and complaining, which can be found in any organization, can affect the moral of those who work with those staff who are always unhappy or mad.

Discussion Questions/Self-Reflection:

1. When you have been around someone who is always unhappy/mad—how do they make you feel?

____

____

____

____

____

____

2. Dr. Whitaker talked about being proactive in dealing with parents through such activities as making positive phone calls or sending home positive notes. Do you do those activities now? If yes—list them and share them with colleagues.

____

____

____

____

____

____

If not—discuss with your colleagues how you/your school can begin such positive activities.

3. What are other ways to be proactive when working difficult students or difficult colleagues?

4. Share your ideas with your team/colleagues. Make a list of activities that can be proactive and help alleviate possible negative situations.

Remember: You can react positively to any situation and create a better environment for you, your students, and your school.

Chapter 8: Building Trust

Key Concepts

1. Building trust with students, parents and colleagues
2. "Zone of Indifference"—a High level of trust

Key Concept 1

Dr. Whitaker discussed the importance of building trust with your students, parents, and colleagues. One example referenced was the use of an Open House before school began to meet and greet parents.

Discussion Questions/Self-Reflection:

1. What are some activities that your school does to develop positive relationships with your students and their parents. List and discuss with your colleagues.

2. Are there other activities/actions you could begin to build positive relationships with your parents and community?

Key Concept 2

Zone of Indifference—A High Level of Trust.

Dr. Whitaker talks about the "*Zone of Indifference*" which is referring to a level of trust. The higher the trust—the larger the *Zone of Indifference.* The larger the *Zone of Indifference* the less you have to defend every action you take.

There are some students who you give a large *Zone of Indifference* because you trust them to do what they say they are going to do. On the flip side, you have students that you question everything they do because of lack of trust.

Discussion Questions/Self-Reflection:

1. How do you build trust with your students regarding their learning?

2. How do you teach students about developing trust?

3. How do you build trust with your colleagues?

4. Select one or more of the techniques discussed regarding trust building with students or with colleagues and incorporate it into your daily/weekly routine. Reflect on how you feel this approach worked for you.

Technique selected:

Response by students:

Remember: Building trust provides a positive impact on your relationship with students, parents, and colleagues.

Chapter 9: Raise the Praise— Minimize the Criticize

Key Concepts

1. Praise should be:

   Immediate

   Authentic

   Specific

   Clean

2. Reinforce a person or action privately

Key Concept 1

Dr. Whitaker stated that his philosophy of life and of education is Raise the Praise—Minimize the Criticize. An example he provide was the use of praise to line up a group of students.

Discussion Questions/Self-Reflection:

1. How often do you feel you use praise in your classroom? List examples to share with your colleagues.

2. How would you describe your student's response to praise?

3. Dr. Whitaker stated that praise should be immediate and specific and clean. What does that mean to you?

4. Do you feel the examples you shared in question 1 meet that criteria?

5. How does your school praise students for their accomplishments?

6. What different activities can you/your school use to praise student achievement/behaviors? Research "best practices" to help develop a positive recognition program.

Note the findings from the research.

Notes

Key Concept 2

Reinforce a person or action privately.

Discussion Questions/Self-Reflection:

1. The last criteria of praise was that you should privately praise a person or his actions. Do you agree with this? List your reasons for why or why not. Share them with your colleagues.

2. Reflect on your discussions with colleagues regarding the use of praise in your classroom. Make an effort to find more actions to praise and less to criticize. Make note of any changes in your classroom atmosphere and your interactions with your students.

Remember: Great teachers understand the power of praise and look for opportunities to praise their students.

Chapter 10: Making It Cool to Care

Key Concepts

1. Develop a Caring Relationship with Students
2. Create a Culture where students and staff are willing to help others.

Key Concept 1

Develop a caring relationship with students.

Research has found that teachers who spend time getting to know their students on a personal level have fewer problems than teachers who do not. This might include discussing favorite hobbies, food, music, etc. The same information could be shared by the teacher with the students. Teachers might share why they chose education as their profession.

Discussion Questions/Self-Reflection:

1. There are many topics to share that are not too personal yet will start to build a bridge with students. Discuss with your colleagues techniques/actions you have used to get to know your students better.

2. Share your ideas and compile a list that others could use in their classrooms.

3. Research proven methods/programs for fostering positive teacher/student relationships and describe your findings.

Notes

Key Concept 2

Create a culture where students and staff are willing to help others.

Discussion Questions/Self-Reflection:

1. Brainstorm some team-building activities that can be used among a group of students or for the school as a whole, such as, the example Dr. Whitaker spoke about in the video—adopting a special needs preschool program.

2. Implement an activity among your students/team/school and reflect on how it made you and your students feel to participate.

Remember: Great Teachers make it Cool to Care about others.

Chapter 11: Great Teachers Make the Difference

Key Concepts

1. Great Teachers Seldom Need to Repair
2. Staying Positive
3. Understand the Impact you have on your Students.

Key Concept 1

Great Teachers seldom need to repair situations as they are always working to repair.

Discussion Questions/Self-Reflection:

1. Dr. Whitaker gave an example of a teacher apologizing to students for having a "bad day" the day before and the students not realizing it had been a bad day for the teacher. Why do you think the students did not realize it?

2. What does Dr. Whitaker mean by "always working to repair"?

Share your thoughts with your team/colleagues.

3. Think of actions you can take to keep from having to repair in your classroom and in relationship with your students and your colleagues. Positive actions I can take include:

4. Implement one or two of those ideas over the next two weeks and describe the impact they had in your classroom.

Remember: Great Teachers work to build a positive climate in their classrooms based on mutual respect and trust.

Key Concept 2

Staying Positive is a critical element to being a Great Teacher.

Dr. Whitaker referred to his "Atta Boy or Atta Girl file" on the video. His suggestion was that you collect articles, letters, a movie, or some other item that could help you refocus if you are having a bad day.

Discussion Questions/Self-Reflection:

1. Do you currently have any articles that you find uplifting? Do you have any letters from students that you have saved? If yes, share the articles with your colleagues to help start a collection of uplifting stories.

2. Start a "Positive Feelings" folder with ideas and suggestions from your colleagues. Continue throughout the year to share new articles as you find them.

3. What other techniques have helped you stay positive when there are stressors which you must deal with? Describe and share these with your colleagues.

4. Dr. Whitaker talked about not giving power to negative people or situations. One example was the letter sent home to all parents regarding picking up their students following a field trip. In this case, the handful of late parents were given the recognition and power over all the parents who were there on time.

Has giving negative power happened in your school or classroom?

If yes—what could be done differently in the future?

5. Have you ever given "negative power" to a student and punished everyone as the result of the actions of one or two students?

If yes, what can you do differently if the same situation arose tomorrow?

Remember: Focus your time and energy on developing and rewarding the positive students.

Key Concept 3

All teachers must understand the impact they have on their students. Dr. Whitaker's file contains letters from his former students in which they talk about the impact he had on their lives.

Discussion Questions/Self-Reflection:

1. If you have taught long enough to have a student(s) write or come back to see you with a similar "Thank You" story—please share it with your group.

2. Did you have a teacher that had an impact on your life—either positive or negative? Describe the impact.

Remember: **Long after a student leaves your classroom, your words and actions could influence decisions they make, how they treat others, and the future they chose. Great Teachers make a positive difference.**

Closing Comments

Dr. Whitaker closes the video with the request that each teacher look at themselves in the mirror each morning and remind themselves that they have chosen the single most important profession there is.

As we come to the end of this workbook, take time to look back over the notes you have made, the tasks, and their outcomes that you set for yourself and the reflections you wrote.

Do you feel you are in the Great Teacher category? Yes or no? Explain.

____

____

____

____

If yes—Congratulations! Your responsibility is to maintain that high level of accomplishment and to assist those teachers who might look to you for help and guidance.

If you don't think you are a Great Teacher yet—think of steps you can take to continue on your journey toward being a Great Teacher.

____

____

____

Using this video and workbook and the "What Great Teacher's Do *Differently*" handbook can provide a foundation for professional growth and improvements in your classroom and school.

Remember: Great Teachers are the most important aspect of a successful school.

Points to Remember

Great Schools begin with Great People. Do your best to be one of the great teachers in your school.

Great Principals help their staff to be Great Teachers and by working together—Great Results will follow.

Great Schools have ALL staff working together for the benefit of their students.

A Great School is full of effective teachers who know how to reach all students.

Great teachers model positive behaviors and have high expectations for themselves as well as for their students.

A Great Teacher has the ability to know how they come across to their students and is always working to improve their effectiveness.

Effective teachers learn from other effective teachers. Use the strengths of your colleagues to learn and grow into a great teacher.

It's how you do what you do that makes the difference in your classroom.

We are the one variable that we have control over in our efforts to improve.

It's often not what you say—but how you say it—that influences the outcome of a conversation.

Believing in your students can help them believe in themselves.

Great teachers always have a plan for learning in their classroom.

Great Teachers expect as much from themselves as they do from their students.

Learning can not take place in an ineffectively managed classroom.

Teachers never know how their actions and words will influence students now and into their future.

Put the emphasis on your best staff and students when determining your decisions.

Focusing on developing a positive attitude and filtering out the negative responses can help create a successful classroom and school environment.

A positive, inviting classroom can set the tone for learning.

You can react positively to any situation and create a better environment for you, your students, and your school.

Building trust provides a positive impact on your relationship with students, parents, and colleagues.

Great teachers understand the power of praise and look for opportunities to praise their students.

Great Teachers make it Cool to Care about others.

Great Teachers work to build a positive climate in their classrooms based on mutual respect and trust.

Focus your time and energy on developing and rewarding positive students.

Long after a student leaves your classroom, your words and actions could influence decisions they make, how they treat others, and the future they choose. Great Teachers make a positive difference.

Great Teachers are the most important aspect of a successful school.

Notes

Journal Notes

If you would like information about inviting Todd Whitaker to speak to your group, please contact him at t-whitaker@indstate.edu or at his web site www.toddwhitaker.com or (812) 237-2904.

Great Quotes for Great Educators

Todd Whitaker and Dale Lumpa

Over 600 insightful, witty nuggets to motivate and inspire you …

… and everyone else at your school.

Teachers—display these quotes in your classrooms!

Administrators—insert them into your faculty memos and share them at staff meetings!

Why is this book unique?

- includes over 100 original quotes from internationally acclaimed speaker and educator Todd Whitaker
- features real quotes from real students, which echo wit and wisdom for educators
- each quote has a direct connection to your life as an educator

Examples of quotes in this book…

"Great teachers have high expectations for their students, but higher expectations for themselves."

Todd Whitaker

"We can never control a classroom until we control ourselves."

Todd Whitaker

2004, 208 pp. paperback 1-903556-82-9 $29.95 plus shipping and handling

Call 888-299-5350 or visit *www.eyeoneducation.com*